# A Beautiful World.

# A Beautiful World.
## Reframing Our Relationship to Creation

By Scott Higgins

ajustcause.com.au

In Association With

micahaustralia.org

Copyright © 2016 Scott Higgins

Title: A Beautiful World. Reframing Our Relationship with Creation

Author: Scott Higgins

ALL RIGHTS RESERVED. This book is copyright. Apart from any fair dealing for the purposes of private study, research, criticism or review, as permitted under the Copyright Act no part of this book may be reproduced or transmitted in any form or by any means, electronic or mechanical, including photocopying, recording, or by any information storage and retrieval system without express written permission from the author/publisher.

Scripture, unless otherwise stated, taken from the New Revised Standard Version Bible: Anglicized Edition, copyright 1989, 1995, Division of Christian Education of the National Council of the Churches of Christ in the United States of America. Used by permission. All rights reserved.

All interior paper stock is acid-free and supplied by a Forest Stewardship Council (FSC) certified provider. We are committed to recycling waste materials resulting from the printing process and only produce units as they are ordered, which reduces excess production.

# Contents

Introduction ........................................................................ 1
The Earth is the Lord's ..................................................... 5
Let Them Have Dominion ............................................ 25
A New Heaven and a New Earth .............................. 43
The Greatest Commandments ...................................... 63
Discussion Guide ............................................................ 75
    Study 1.  The Earth is the Lord's ............................................ 77
    Study 2.  Let Them Have Dominion ...................................... 83
    Study 3.  A New Heavens and Earth ..................................... 87
    Study 4.  The Greatest Commandments ............................... 91

# Introduction

It was on a camping trip in Halls Gap, Victoria, that I saw my first wild koala. I had seen plenty of koalas in zoos, but had long wanted to come across one in its natural habitat. My wife, Sandy, was taking a shower and I was lying in our tent when I heard a loud grunting sound. Thinking it was a wild pig I, somewhat foolishly, set off to find it. As I got closer the grunting grew louder and I realised it was emanating from somewhere up in the trees! Unless there had been a dramatic mutation in the pigs at Halls Gap I was not hunting a pig. I had no idea that koalas could make such a loud, aggressive sound!

Experiences like this have always thrilled me, so it was disturbing to read World Wide Fund For Nature's (WWF) 2016 Living Planet Report. This contained the news that between 1970 and 2012 the number of wild animals on the earth declined by 58%. That's over half the world's animal populations gone during my lifetime and on current trends it will be two-thirds by 2020. The causes are almost entirely due to human action. If there was ever a sign that we are having a deleterious impact on the planet this is it.

Scientists tell us that we have entered the age of "the Anthropocene". By this they mean that humankind is now the dominant force shaping the environmental systems of the earth. This is not good news, for we are pushing many of the planet's key systems to breaking point, demanding more of the earth than it can sustainably provide.

Of all people, Christians should have something positive and powerful to say in response to this, for we affirm that the world and its creatures are the creation of God. Yet many Christians have a theological heritage that has minimised the earth and earth care. We have imagined that our true self is located in our spirit and that our eternal home is the immaterial realm of heaven. God's interest is in us, not the creation nor the other living creatures.

This book argues that we need to reframe our relationship to creation. It calls for recognition that God has plans, purposes and love for the earth and its creatures that extend beyond any benefit they hold for human beings; that a key part of our human purpose is not to lord it over the planet and other creatures but to serve their interests and seek their flourishing; and that the entire creation is the object of God's saving work. This provides a framework for integrating care for creation into the heart of discipleship.

There are three ways this book can be used:

## As a preaching guide.

The four chapters of the book could form the basis of a four-part sermon series. Each chapter focuses on a dimension of a Christian engagement with creation and concludes with an eco-concern (an area of environmental concern) and an eco-discipline (a simple way of applying the teaching of the chapter). A helpful way to proceed would be to present the eco-concern separate from the sermon and devote it to prayer, and to conclude each service by asking people to implement the eco-discipline for the week.

## As a Bible study guide.

At the end of the book you will find a small group discussion guide. It is written in such a way that people do not need to read the accompanying chapter, although they will get more from the study if they do. It is recommended that in weeks 2-4 members of the group report back on how they found the eco-discipline for the week.

## For personal growth.

Simply read through the book and implement the eco-disciplines for yourself.

# Chapter 1

# The Earth is the Lord's

Of all the fish in the world, the Frillfin Goby is one of the least interesting, or so you might be tempted to think. Found in rock pools that dot coastlines across the world, at just 10 centimetres long it's not going to impress anybody with its size. Its flat head and mottled brown colours are not going to dazzle anybody with their beauty. This small fish, does however, have one extraordinary quality. It possesses the ability to launch itself out of the rockpool in which it lives, through the air and into a nearby rockpool. In fact, when threatened by a predator, the Frillfin Goby can leap from rockpool to rockpool to rockpool until it reaches the safety of the ocean.

Think about that for a moment and you realise just how astonishing it is. When the Frillfin Goby makes that leap it is unsighted. How does it know where to jump? Is it just dumb luck that it lands in another rock pool? No, the Frillfin Goby hits its target every time. Scientists believe that when the tide comes in and covers the rocks the Frillfin Goby swims over the area and memorises the terrain. When the tide goes out and the Goby is once again restricted to a rockpool it calculates its leap from memory.[1]

This little fish challenges centuries of Christian thinking about creation. From the time of the church fathers (2nd and 3rd century) through to the present, Christians have believed that God created the earth and its creatures solely to serve human need. One third century church leader, Origen, taught that

> *The Creator, then, has constituted all things the servants of the rational being and of his natural understanding. For some purposes we require dogs, say as guardians of our sheep-folds, or of our cattle-yards, or goat-pastures, or of our dwellings; and for other purposes we need oxen, as for agriculture; and for others, again, we make use of those which bear the yoke, or beasts of burden. And so it may be said that the race of lions, and bears, and leopards, and wild boars, and such like, has been given to us in order to call into exercise the elements of the manly character that exists within us.*[2]

Origen is so convinced that all things are created for human benefit that not only domesticated animals are seen to serve humankind but so are the lion, the bear and the leopard. They exist to draw out human courage. This view persisted throughout church history. When we open 16th century reformer John Calvin's commentary on Genesis we find this reflection on 1:26-28:

> *[God] appointed man, it is true, lord of the world...and his authority was not given to Adam only, but to all his posterity as well as to him. And hence we infer what was the end for which all things were created; namely, that none of the conveniences and necessaries of life might be wanting to men.³*

The idea that everything was created to serve humankind continues into the modern era. In the respected and widely used Word commentary on Genesis, Gordon Wenham argued that in Genesis 1:

> *Man is the apex of the created order: the whole narrative moves towards the creation of man. Everything is made for the man's benefit.⁴*

If this theological tradition is correct, how do we explain the existence of the extraordinarily clever Frillfin Goby? The fish does not have any known benefit to humankind. It is not a source of food for human beings, nor, to the best of our knowledge, is it a keystone species that is critical to the functioning of an ecosystem. The Goby could join the myriad of species that have become extinct and few of us would notice its passing.

Could it be that the Frillfin Goby points us to a deeper and richer theology of creation?

# Taking Genesis Back from Aristotle and the Stoics

"Aristotle and the Stoics" sounds like the name of a rock band, but is in fact a reference to two schools of philosophy that were very influential in the life of the early church. These philosophies argued that the rational, or "higher", forms or life were to be served by the irrational, or "lower", forms of life. This became part of the worldview of our theologians, who then read the biblical accounts of creation through that lens. The climactic point of the creation story was seen to be the creation of human beings and the conclusion was drawn that everything created before humankind was created for humankind.

At the time of the Renaissance this anthropocentric interpretation of the creation stories was allied to the view that human beings should not only use creation as it was, but should transform and develop it, bend it to our will, and make it the servant of human progress.[5] Theologians started to speak of the image of God as the capacity to control nature. Where theologians in the premodern period had emphasised that humankind was part of creation, the emphasis was now on humankind's difference from nature. In this way Christian theology became the handmaiden of the determination to conquer nature that until very recently marked the modern world.

Certainly, humankind is a strong focus within the story of

creation. More space is devoted to the description of our creation than to that of other creatures; it is only before forming human beings that God deliberates ("let us make humankind…"); humankind alone is created as God's image and commissioned to rule the animals and subdue the earth; and the world is clearly designed to be hospitable to humankind. It is one thing, however, to say that humankind is an important focus of the creation story, and another to say that it is the primary focus. Richard Bauckham points out that:

> *the account is not anthropocentric [i.e. human centred] but theocentric [i.e. God centred]. Its climax is not the creation of humans on the sixth day, but God's Sabbath rest, God's enjoyment of God's completed work on the seventh day (Gen. 2:2). Creation exists for God's glory.*[6]

Both the structure and the content of Genesis 1 point to this conclusion. Structurally there is a neat symmetry between days 1-3 and days 4-6. On the first three days God creates the physical structures of the world and on days 4-6 they are filled with their corresponding elements. The creation of humankind on day six does not stand apart from the previous acts of creation but in continuity with them. It is day seven that stands apart.

## STRUCTURE OF GENESIS 1

| Day 1: Night and day | Day 4: Sun, moon & stars |
|---|---|
| Day 2: Waters and Sky | Day 5: Sea creatures and birds |
| Day 3: Land and vegetation | Day 6: Land animals and humankind |

Day 7: Blessing and rest

Why have we not recognised the significance of day seven? Old Testament scholar John Walton argues that those of us who live within a western context miss a critical clue that would not have been missed by the original ancient near-eastern audience. This clue would have led them to identify day seven as the stunning climax of the creation story.

> *In the traditional view…day seven is mystifying. It appears to be nothing more than an afterthought with theological concerns about Israelites observing the Sabbath – an appendix, a postscript, a tack on.*
>
> *In contrast, a reader from the ancient world would know immediately what was going on and recognise the role of day seven. Without hesitation the ancient reader would conclude that this is a temple text and that day seven is the most important of the seven days.*

> *... How could reactions be so different? The difference is the piece of information that everyone knew in the ancient world and to which most modern readers are totally oblivious: divinity rests in a temple, and only in a temple.*
>
> *...The most central truth to the creation account is that this world is a place for God's presence.*[7]

To argue that the earth is the temple of God places the events of days 1 to 6 in a new frame. Rather than God creating a world in which everything is centered on the needs of humankind, God creates a world perfectly fit for his presence. It's dazzling array of landscapes, underwater vistas and living creatures sing to his creativity and glory and bring him joy and delight. God's provision for the need of every creature, from the fish in the depths of the oceans, to the animals that inhabit the highest mountains, and to humankind, are a celebration of the impulse to love that is at the heart of God's nature. Each element of creation signals the unrivalled majesty of the Creator.

This theme is picked up and developed in the Psalms. The writer of Psalm 8 is overwhelmed by the majesty of God displayed in creation. Psalm 19 celebrates the way the heavens point to the greatness and glory of God, and do so without fail day after day and night after night. Psalm 24 calls us to live in light of the fact that the earth and everything in it belong to God; Psalm 104 rejoices in God's providential care for all creatures and marvels at the dazzling array of life God created. These realities signal God's wisdom and power, and bring God joy. Psalm 148 calls not just humankind but all creation to offer praise to God. Indeed the very last sentence in the book of Psalms is a call for everything that has breath to praise the Lord (Psalm 150:6).

Commenting on Psalm 148, Leslie Allen notes that

> *Just as a fine piece of craftsmanship brings glory to its craftsman, so the destiny of the created world is to glorify Yahweh* [i.e., Israel's God] *by reflecting his divine power. By fulfilling their divinely allotted functions, the works of the celestial creation exist as eloquent witnesses to his self-revelation through them.*[8]

The notion of the world as God's temple is prominent in Isaiah. Isaiah 6 relates the commissioning of the prophet. Isaiah has a vision in which he sees the Lord seated on a throne that fills earth and sky, in which the hem of God's robe fills the Jerusalem temple. The Jerusalem temple, which served as a sign of God's presence with Israel, cannot contain the presence of God. In chapter 40 the prophet brings good news that Israel is to return from exile. He is the God who measures the oceans in the hollow of his hand and the heavens with the breadth of his hand (verse 12); who sits enthroned above the earth and stretches out the heavens like a tent in which to live (verse 22). In the final chapter God declares he needs no house (ie temple) built for him, for the world is his temple:

> *Thus says the Lord:*
>
> *Heaven is my throne*
>
> *and the earth is my footstool;*
>
> *what is the house that you would build for me,*
>
> *and what is my resting-place?*
>
> *All these things my hand has made,*
>
> *and so all these things are mine,*
>
> *says the Lord.* Isaiah 66:1-2

The closing chapters of the Bible sees that which is currently perceived by faith – God's presence in the world – gloriously realised in the tangible experience of humankind. God inhabits the new heavens and new earth, his dwelling place among the people (Revelation 21:1-24). The creation vision is finally accomplished, God in his world temple enjoying the worship of creation and bringing hope, healing and life to humankind.

The New Testament letters focus the theme of creation wide worship on Christ. Colossians 1:15-20 declares that not only were all things created through Christ but they were created for Christ, who will reconcile all things to himself. Philippians 2 reminds us that all things, "in heaven and on earth and under the earth" were created to worship Christ as Lord. Ephesians 1:10 declares that God's purpose in history is to bring all things to a point of completion, unity and harmony under the leadership of Christ.

………………………………………………………………..………

If it be true that the purpose of creation is to be the temple of God, a place in which God dwells, and in which all things signal God's glory, we will abandon the notion that everything God created needs to be of value to human beings. In Genesis 1 land animals are divided into three categories – livestock, animals that crawl on the ground, and wild animals. Only the first was of any use to the ancient Israelites, who were the original recipients of the creation stories. Creeping animals were deemed unclean and wild animals were dangerous. Yet in Genesis 1 they are all part of the rich and varied complex of life forms that declare God's majesty and are a focus of his love.

Or consider "the great sea monsters" of Genesis 1:21. Chief among these was a creature the Old Testament knows as "leviathan" (Psalm 104:26). Human domination of the world is now so complete that it is difficult to imagine a past in which many habitats lay beyond human reach and many animals beyond human control. Yet in the biblical era creation was filled with places inaccessible to humankind and with animals that represented danger. No creature was more dangerous than the "Leviathan", a name given for a fierce, large and uncontrollable creature of the sea – possibly a great whale or crocodile. Its fearsome attributes are described poetically in Job 41:

> *Can you fill its skin with harpoons,*
> *or its head with fishing-spears?*
> *Lay hands on it;*

*think of the battle; you will not do it again!*
*Any hope of capturing it will be disappointed;*
*were not even the gods overwhelmed at the sight of it?*
*No one is so fierce as to dare to stir it up.*
*Who can stand before it?*
*Who can confront it and be safe?*
*—under the whole heaven, who?*
Job 41:7-11

The Leviathan may have been frightful to humankind but in Genesis 1 "the great sea monsters" are part of the creation brought into being by God, declared good, and commissioned to multiply and fill the seas. In Psalm 148 they are included in the call to creation to join in praise of God. And in Psalm 104 the Leviathan was formed by God "to frolic" in the oceans. It is one of a multitude of creatures that lay beyond the reach of humanity but that were part of a global community of creatures sustained and enjoyed by their divine Father. The biblical authors saw no need to identify the value of Leviathan in relation to humankind, but saw this terrifying creature as an expression of the greatness and power of God and a source of joy for the Creator.

In this world not only the Leviathan but the Frillfin Goby makes sense. It need not serve human interest at all, but has value as an expression of the creative power of God that brings joy to God with each leap from one rock pool to the next, and is the object of God's great love.

..................................................................................

# Loved by God

To say everything was created for God's glory does not mean the planet and its creatures are playthings in the hands of a capricious God, or that their interests are of no concern. On the contrary, God is a Trinity of love that is extended outward in pursuit of the well-being of all things. This means that God's love is poured out not only on human beings but upon all creation. It is no surprise then, that the first covenant God makes is with Noah and his family, all animals and the earth (Genesis 9) and that the new covenant God promises to make brings together Israel "with the wild animals, the birds of the air, and the creeping things of the ground" (Hosea 2:16-19).

Jesus spoke of God's provision for the birds of the air and the flowers of the field (Matthew 6:19–34), insisting that not even a sparrow falls from the sky apart from the will of its loving Creator.

> *Are not two sparrows sold for a penny? Yet not one of them will fall to the ground unperceived by your Father. And even the hairs of your head are all counted. So do not be afraid; you are of more value than many sparrows. (Matthew 10:29-31)*

Jesus drew attention to the sparrow because it was the least valued bird in the marketplace, the food source of the very poor. To Jesus, not even this most overlooked of birds was overlooked by God. Even the sparrow was the object of

God's care.

Similar ideas are found at the end of Job. In three stunning chapters we're exposed to God's work in the world. God called the universe into being, commands the weather, and provides for the animals. At times the images are of God's great power and, at other times, of God's tenderness:

> *Do you know when the mountain goats give birth? Do you watch when the doe has her fawn? Do you count the months till they give birth? Do you know the time they give birth?* Job 39:1-2

The tone is not merely factual, but filled with hope and longing. God is counting down the months, eagerly awaiting the arrival of a newborn fawn and kid. Here is a God deeply engaged with creation.

God's great love for all living things sees them assigned their spaces on the earth and God providing for their sustenance (Psalm 104). We live in an era in which we invade a myriad of ecological niches, almost no habitat is beyond us, and our technological and intellectual superiority over the other creatures allow us to simply take what they need and indeed, when we wish it, to take them for our use. But this is a recent development. Psalm 104 has a sense that the Earth is a shared space for all creatures. The first section of the psalm (verses 1–13) celebrates the ways God has ordered the world so that it is rich with water that quenches the thirst of creatures. The middle part of the psalm (verses 14-30) celebrates the ways that God provides for the creatures of the Earth. God provides food sources such as grass for cattle, plants for humankind, and prey for lions; spaces for the creatures to dwell, such as trees for the birds, mountains for the goats, crags for the coneys; God even provides night and day to mark off the times creatures do their hunting.

# Living on God's Earth

Our study suggests we need to reframe our approach to creation. In the biblical outlook the world is created as the temple of God. The mountains, forests, oceans, living creatures, and human beings exist as an expression of the beauty, majesty, wisdom, and greatness of God, and find their highest purpose in praise of their Creator. All living creatures, human and nonhuman, find their home in this temple, where they are the focus of God's loving care, a source of God's joy, and derive their value and meaning from their relation to God.

## Worship

If the world is God's temple, we have the opportunity to know, love and worship the God who inhabits it, and creation helps us do this. In the beauty of the sunset we will see reflected the beauty of God; in the vastness of the universe, we will see reflected the greatness of God; in the tender embrace of husband-and-wife or parent-and-child we will see reflected the tenderness of God.

Some may object that this sentimentalises creation. They point to the fact that creation is often the place for and cause of pain and suffering. Orcas play with seals, tossing them backwards and forwards through the air, before killing them; tsunamis destroy infrastructure and take lives; mutant genes create cancers that slowly kill. Why do we not take these to be signs that the Creator is cruel or indifferent?

The witness of creation is ambiguous apart from God's revelation to us in the Scriptures and supremely in Jesus. This revelation identifies God as loving, gracious and kind. It sees the world as good - so that it reflects the character and purposes of God - but also broken and in need of healing. In this sense the presence of suffering in the universe functions as a sign of the need for creation to be made whole. Yet, at the same time, the lens of faith allows us to celebrate all that is good in the world as signs of the character and love of God and to draw us into worship.

## Respect

If the world is God's temple, creation is designed to reflect the glory of God, and all living things are the objects of God's love and joy, we will treat creation as valuable and the lives of all living things as morally significant.

A theocentric approach does not suggest that all living

creatures have the same value. In Genesis 9 humankind is granted permission to consume animals, but because humankind is created in the image of God, it is not permitted to take human life (Genesis 9:1-6). Likewise, while the Bible envisages the redemption of all creation, including the animal world (eg Isaiah 11:1-11; 65:17-25), it speaks only of the resurrection of human beings. That is, where the Bible speaks of animals as part of the new heavens and earth, it does not appear that this will include my pet cat resurrected from the dead.

But to say that we do not attach the same value to the life of a spider or a bird that we do to a human, is not to say we attach no value to them, or value them only to the degree they serve our interest. Rather we will recognise that all living creatures in their own way reflect the glory and majesty of their Creator, sing praise to their Creator, and are loved by their Creator. We should therefore be concerned about them; recognise that the earth is to be shared with them; and treat them with kindness, compassion and care.

## Eco-concern: Cruelty to Animals

A biblical theology of creation calls us to a new way of engaging with non-human living creatures. Genesis appears to assume the human diet was originally vegetarian: Genesis 1:29-30 sees God granting humankind the vegetation but not animals for food, and it is not until Genesis 9 that humankind is granted animals as a food source. In Isaiah's vision of the new heavens and earth (Isaiah 11:6-9; 65:25), the fear that marked the relation between humankind and animals once the animals become a food source for human beings (Genesis 9:2-3) has ceased and presumably predation with it. At creation and new creation the animals have the almost singular purpose of bearing witness to God's glory, bringing joy to God, and enjoying God's love.

In the present however we also use animals for human benefit. We use animals for food, for sport, for product testing, and for companionship. The number of animals involved is staggering. In 2015 594 million chickens, 19 million cattle, 31 million sheep and 5 million pigs were slaughtered in Australia.[9] In 2013 there were estimated to be more than 25 million pets in Australia.[10]

An anthropocentric approach values the welfare of these animals only to the degree they serve human interest. If, for example, the most economically profitable way to rear pigs involves pain or suffering for the pigs, this is acceptable. A theocentric approach counters that at the same time we use animals as a resource for our benefit, we must also treat them with respect and kindness. A helpful guideline to what this means is the RSPCA's identification of five freedoms animals should enjoy[11]:

> *Freedom from hunger and thirst: by ready access to fresh water and a diet to maintain full health and vigour.*
>
> *Freedom from discomfort: by providing an appropriate*

*environment including shelter and a comfortable resting area.*

*Freedom from pain, injury or disease: by prevention through rapid diagnosis and treatment.*

*Freedom to express normal behaviour: by providing sufficient space, proper facilities and company of the animal's own kind.*

*Freedom from fear and distress: by ensuring conditions and treatment which avoid mental suffering.*

Using these measures the RSPCA finds that these principles are commonly violated in the

- farming industry, in the caging of hens and the export of live animals such as cattle and sheep to countries that use brutal slaughtering methods;
- recreational industries, in the use of whips in horse racing; use of live baits, overbreeding, and high rates of injury in greyhound racing; and high levels of injuries to horses that is inherent to jumps racing;
- cosmetics industry, in the use of animals for product testing;
- in the pet industry, in the operation of some puppy farms.

A theocentric approach rejects the infliction of pain and suffering on animals. This will mean abandoning some practices as simply incompatible with kindness; modifying practices so that they do not inflict pain or suffering; and developing new practices that allow animals to be treated humanely at the same time we use them for human goods.

You can contribute to change in this area by using the RSPCA's shophumane.org.au website to inform your shopping habits and by participating in advocacy campaigns run by groups such as the RSPCA and World Wide Find (WWF).

## Eco-discipline: Celebration

Take time each day to focus upon a particular part of creation – it could be a sunrise, a tree, or even a pet. Reflect upon the ways this part of creation points you to God, brings joy to God, and how you should value it, given it is the creation of God.

# Chapter 2

# Let Them Have Dominion

*The Purpose Driven Life*, written by American pastor Rick Warren, was one of the best-selling Christian books of the last twenty years. The promotional blurb on the back claims

> *This book will help you understand why you are alive and God's amazing plan for you – both here and now, and for eternity... Knowing God's purpose for creating you will reduce your stress, focus your energy, simplify your decisions, give meaning to your life, and, most important, prepare you for eternity.*[12]

The book offers five purposes for our lives: to bring pleasure to God; to belong to God's family; to become like Christ; to serve God; and to engage in mission to the world.

In the section on mission Warren inspires us:

> *You were made for a mission. God is at work in the world, and he wants you to join him. This assignment is called your mission.*[13]

Yet as he unpacks God's mission there is nothing about God's work with creation, and nothing calling us to join God in the work of caring for creation. Warren is not alone in this. Christian exposition of the meaning of our lives often focuses on our relation to God and our fellow human beings, but rarely on our relation to the earth and its creatures. Yet when we go to the Bible's creation stories we discover that a central part of our life purpose is to steward creation.

The creation stories of Genesis 1 and 2 are important texts, for origins stories help us define who we are, our place in the universe, and the core of what it means for us to be human. In both stories - the story of God creating the world over six days and the story of the Garden of Eden - caring for creation is a key rationale for human existence. This is much more than saying Christians should care for the environment. I am arguing that the creation texts understand this purpose as being at the very core of what it means to be human.

## God's Representatives

In the first creation story human beings are part of creation, yet have a distinctive function within it. Humans and the creatures of the sea, sky and land share creaturely status, including the command to be fruitful, multiply and fill the earth. Unlike the rest of God's creatures, however, humankind alone is created in the image and likeness of God and given responsibility to "subdue the Earth" and "rule over the fish in the sea and the birds in the sky and over every living creature that moves on the ground".

There was a time when these words were celebrated. The Renaissance gave rise to the notion that to be human was to be the master of the world, to bend and shape nature to our will. But in our ecologically aware age how can we credibly speak of "ruling" and "subduing"?

Some scholars suggest we need to reject this language. Norman Habel, for example, argues that Genesis 1:1-25 tells the Earth story, and that this conflicts with the human story introduced in verses 26-28. The Earth story proclaims a good earth, whereas the human story speaks of the need to master and subjugate the earth. We need to reject the human story and listen to the earth story.[14] While I applaud the sensitivity of Norman Habel and others to the concerns of the planet and its creatures, I think the language of Genesis 1:26-28 remains important. Yes, the phrasing is confronting, but it reminds us that humankind wields enormous power over the earth and its creatures, and that the spread of humankind across the earth has meant we have transformed it. The act of living requires food to be cultivated, harvested, cooked and consumed; clothes to be made; homes, hospitals, schools and roads to be constructed. Production and supply of these always involves the imposition of our will upon the environment. We cut, tear, dig, grow, harvest and transform the planet. Genesis 1 calls our attention to this, but frames it as a mandate to care, not exploit.

There are two keys to making sense of Genesis 1 for our world today. First, to disentangle ourselves from centuries of anthropocentric readings of the text that make humankind the focus of creation and define the value of the earth and its creatures solely in terms of their benefit to humankind. As we saw in chapter 1, Genesis 1 is better read as identifying the earth as the dwelling place of God in which all things find their meaning and value in relation to their Creator. Whatever we might say about ruling and subduing it has this in mind.

The second key is to remember that in the Bible ruling and power are always to be focused in service of others.

In Genesis 1:26-28 the exhortations to rule and subdue are found both immediately before and immediately after the description of humankind being made in God's image. This has been interpreted in many ways, but the most widely held view among biblical scholars is that the image designated humankind the representative of God on earth.[15] The idea that a human being could image God was not unique to ancient Israel. This concept is found in the texts of ancient Egypt and Assyria, but with one critical difference. In the Egyptian and Assyrian texts the king alone is described as the image of God. This designated the king as God's representative on the earth. Genesis takes this familiar idea and applies it to all people. Gordon Wenham comments that

> *It appears that the OT has democratised this old idea. It affirms that not just a king, but every man and woman, bears God's image and is his representative on earth.*[16]

Given the regal context, it is not surprising to find the language of ruling and subduing, for this is what kings do. The critical question then becomes the manner in which we rule the animals and subdue the earth. Given we do this as representatives of God, we would be wise to consider the manner of God's rule of the animals and God's subduing of the earth.

Let us first take up the issue of subduing the earth. The cultures around Israel told creation myths that saw the creation come into being as the result of conflict between competing gods. Nahum Sarna comments that

> *They inevitably regard the achievement of world order as the outgrowth of an overwhelming exhibition of power on the part of one god who, through a monopoly of violence, manages to impose his will upon all others.*[17]

In one of the more famous of these pagan mythologies, the god Marduk triumphs over the god Tiamat, and forms the heavens and the earth by slicing Tiamat in two.

By contrast, in Genesis 1, the earth begins as a formless void covered by water. God then separates different dimensions of this watery mass to create a life-friendly planet. Night is separated from day; the waters above from the waters below; land from sea; until a planet fit for life emerges. God's subduing of the earth is not about violent triumph over enemies, but is the ordering of creation so that it is life-giving to all his creatures.

...................................................................................

The same reality is described in more poetic form in Psalm 104 as the process by which God covered the earth with water ("the deep"), and then through his rebuke forced the waters to flow to their appropriate places. Once in their appropriate places the waters were able to function as sources of nourishment for the earth's vegetation and its living creatures.

As God's representatives we are to take our cue from God. We subdue the earth by arranging and ordering it in such a way that it nourishes and sustains life. This includes our own lives and the lives of all other creatures.

Similarly, when we ask how it is God rules over the animals, the answer seems to be that he creates spaces for them to dwell and provides resources for their flourishing (Psalm 104; Matthew 6:25-34).

When we step back from the question of God's rule of the earth and the animals, and consider the broader theme of power and rule, the Bible consistently argues that power is to be used to secure the well-being of others. This is true of God's rule of humankind.

In Acts 17:24-27 the apostle Paul argues that God's relation to humankind is not driven by a need for human beings to provide him sustenance. Rather it is God who sustains living creatures. The purpose of God's actions towards human beings is that they would reach out and find him. In Matthew 5:43-48 Jesus comments that God's reign is characterised by love even for his enemies. God sends sunshine and rain, essential to the success of the small scale farming communities Jesus addressed, on his friend and his enemy.

If this is how God rules, it is also how human authorities should rule. The book of Proverbs closes with a remarkable call to King Lemuel:

> *It is not for kings, O Lemuel,*
> *it is not for kings to drink wine,*
> *or for rulers to desire strong drink,*
> *or they will drink and forget what has been decreed,*
> *and will pervert the rights of all the afflicted...*
>
> *Speak out for those who cannot speak,*
> *for the rights of all the destitute.*
> *Speak out, judge righteously,*
> *defend the rights of the poor and needy.*
> Proverbs 31:1-9

Lemuel was to remember that his power was not to be used to indulge himself, but to secure justice for the very least members of his society.

In Jeremiah 22 we see this principle expressed in the contrast between King Josiah and his son Shallum.

> *"Woe to him who builds his palace by unrighteousness,*
> *his upper rooms by injustice, making his countrymen*
> *work for nothing, not paying them for their labour. He*
> *says, 'I will build myself a great palace with spacious*

> *upper rooms.' So he makes large windows in it, panels it with cedar and decorated in red. Does it make you a king to have more and more cedar? Did not your father have food and drink? He did what was right and just, so all went well with him. He defended the cause of the poor and needy, and so all went well. Is that not what it means to know me?" declares the Lord.*
> Jeremiah 22:13-16

Shallum used his power to exploit the people for his own gain. Josiah did the opposite. He used his power to secure the cause of the poor and needy.

The good king is the servant king, a theme developed not only in the Old Testament, but in the example and teaching of Jesus.

> *You know that the rulers of the Gentiles lord it over them, and their high officials exercise authority over them. Not so with you. Instead whoever wants to become great among you must be your servant, and whoever wants to be first must be your slave – just as the son of man did not come to be served, but to serve and to give his life as a ransom for many.* Matthew 20:25-28

There is, then, a continual theme throughout the Bible that ruling is about service. If applied to Genesis 1:26–28, it suggests that our calling is to secure the well-being of all the creatures of the earth.

The image that emerges from Genesis 1 is that God

created a planet filled with a diverse array of creatures as a place in which he delights to dwell. Human beings serve as his representatives to the rest of creation, working the earth and its resources so that the life of all creatures is sustained.

# God's Gardeners

This reading is reinforced by the second creation story, which begins by telling us that

> *no shrub of the field had yet appeared on the earth and no plant of the field had yet sprung up, for the Lord God had not sent rain on the earth and there was no human to work the ground.* Genesis 2:5-6

For many years I skipped over this, assuming that the world in which God planted the garden was the developed world of Genesis 1. It seems, however, that Genesis 2 is telling the creation story all over again from an alternate point of view. Where the starting point for the first story was a watery chaos ("the Earth was formless and void") here the starting point is a planet that is barren, perhaps calling to mind the idea of desert.

Upon this barren planet, devoid of vegetation, unfit for habitation by humans or animals, God plants a garden. It is an oasis complete with trees that are pleasing to the eye and good for food, and rivers that ensure it stays lush and well-watered. The first human was crafted from the dust of the barren earth outside the garden, made a living being and placed in the garden with a very specific job: to till and keep it.

We have already been told that the reason vegetation had not sprung up outside the garden was the lack of water and the lack of somebody to till the ground. Inside the garden both are present, meaning the trees that provide food and are pleasing to the eye can continue to flourish. Alongside tilling, the human is to "keep" the garden. Elsewhere in the Bible this is often translated as "guard", which begs the question, what is the human guarding against? The most obvious conclusion would be the barren earth outside the garden. Without tilling the garden will devolve into an uninhabitable space, and the reverse also holds true. As humankind multiplies and spreads outward, tilling turns the barren earth into garden.

Humanity's role is to be the groundskeeper, serving God's vision that the earth be transformed from desert into garden.

# Caretakers in the World of Genesis 3-11

The Old Testament is focused on the story of God's dealings with Israel, a story that commences in Genesis 12 with the call of Abraham. Genesis 1-11 is an introduction that sets the scene for what follows. Genesis 1 tells of the creation of the world and is followed by three stories of decline - the Garden (Genesis 2-4); the flood (Genesis 6-9); and the Tower of Babel (Genesis 11) - connected by genealogies (Genesis 5; 10; 11:10-25).

The genealogies show the command to be fruitful and multiply being fulfilled. Humankind does spread across the earth. The stories show that instead of filling the earth with communities of love, justice and grace and stewarding the planet so that all living things enjoy the provision of God, humankind descends into selfishness, pride, and violence. Adam and Eve eat the fruit because they believe it will give them knowledge that rivals God's. They do gain new understanding, but they also turn against each other and are expelled from the Garden (Genesis 3). Cain usurps the prerogative of God over life and death, only to find himself banished from the land (Genesis 4). In the period preceding the flood, "the sons of God" marry "the daughters of men", which is traditionally interpreted to mean human beings intermarried with angelic beings, presumably in an effort to attain godlike powers (Genesis 6:1-4). All they succeed in doing is turning the earth into a place of violence (Genesis 6:5-8). The tower builders in the Plain of Shinar believe they are able to reach the place of the gods and so dominate those around them, but all they receive is confusion and division. (Genesis 11:1-10).

The relationship between humankind and the other living creatures is marked by fear, violence and predation (Genesis 3:14-16; 9:1-6) and harnessing the productivity of the earth becomes difficult (Genesis 3:17-19). Human rule of the earth ceased to focus on seeking the well-being of all creation, and turned instead to a narrow and violent attempt to use the earth and its resources to serve human delusions of power.

Herein lie the seeds of the environmental destruction we are wreaking on the planet and other living creatures.

## Reclaiming our Vocation

In Genesis 12 God begins the work of restoring blessing to creation. God promises Abram that

> *I will make of you a great nation, and I will bless you, and make your name great, so that you will be a blessing. I will bless those who bless you, and the one who curses you I will curse; and in you all the families of the earth shall be blessed.* Genesis 12:2-3

It is noteworthy that "the families of the earth" likely refers not only to human families but to all living creatures. Just a few chapters earlier, after the flood waters subsided, God commanded Noah to

> *Bring out with you every living thing that is with you of all flesh—birds and animals and every creeping thing that creeps on the earth—so that they may abound on the earth, and be fruitful and multiply on the earth.' So Noah went out with his sons and his wife and his sons' wives. And every animal, every creeping thing, and every*

*bird, everything that moves on the earth, went out of the ark by* **families**. Genesis 8:16-19

The word translated "families" in the commissioning to Abraham is the same word used for the animals in Genesis 8. With Abraham God is beginning his work of restoring blessing to all creation, which includes humankind recovering its responsibility to steward creation to wholeness.[18]

As surely as we understand part of our personal mission in life is to know and worship God; as surely as we understand that part of our purpose in life is to help people come to know Christ and build communities of loving justice; so we understand that part of the very reason God put us here on this planet is to steward it, to ensure that its life flourishes. And not just human life, but all life. Using the planet's resources in a sustainable fashion; conserving habitat so the various species of life on earth can continue to flourish; and treating all living things with compassion and care, is fundamental to who we are created to be.

## Eco-concern: Biodiversity

The World Wide Fund for Nature's 2016 Living Planet Index shows that the number of animals living in the wild declined by 58% between 1970 and 2012, and that the trajectory is for even more to be lost.[19] It's worth turning that figure over in your mind. In the space of one lifetime the number of animals living in the wild has more than halved!

The primary drivers are over-exploitation and habitat loss/degradation, along with climate change, introduction of invasive species and pollution.[20] Over-exploitation refers to taking resources from the earth at such a pace that animal and plant populations are not able to reproduce quickly enough to replace those that are lost. Logging, hunting and over-fishing are the biggest culprits.[21] With respect to habitat loss, the biggest contributing factor is land used for farming crops and livestock.[22] A sense of the enormity of these impacts is driven home when thinking about habitat loss in Australia. In the last 200 years Australia has lost 75% of its rainforests and nearly 50% of all forests; over 60% of coastal wetlands in southern and eastern parts of the country; and nearly 90% of temperate woodlands and mallee.[23]

Not only are wild animal populations in decline, but many scientists believe we are experiencing the world's sixth great extinction event.[24] On five previous occasions the bulk of species on earth have become extinct. Today we are witnessing extinctions at 1,000-10,000 times the rate that would occur were it not for human impacts. What makes this extinction event different from the past is the rapid pace at which it is occurring and that humankind is the cause.

> *Of all the plant, amphibian, reptile, bird and mammal species that have gone extinct since AD 1500, 75% were harmed by overexploitation or agricultural activity or both*

*(often in combination with the introduction of invasive alien species). Climate change will become an increasingly dominant problem in the biodiversity crisis. But human development and population growth mean that the impacts of overexploitation and agricultural expansion will also increase.*[25]

Just as diminishing biodiversity has disconcerting detrimental effects, so the restoration of biodiversity can have astonishing positive effects. Almost 70 years after they became extinct from Yellowstone National Park, wolves were reintroduced in 1995. The impact astonished observers. When the wolves departed, elk populations grew, spread into areas they had previously not occupied, and rather than moving on during the winter, grazed heavily on young Willow, Aspen and Cottonwood plants. This led to a decline in the Beaver population which depended upon willows to survive the winter. The reintroduction of the wolf meant that the Elk moved along during the winter periods, which allowed the willow stands to recover, and has seen the return of Beavers to Yellowstone. This in turn has had substantial positive effects upon the streams. Other species have also begun to thrive, including bears, birds of prey, beetles and cats such as the lynx. You can view an inspiring video that tells the story at https://www.youtube.com/watch?v=ysa5OBhXz-Q.

To combat declining biodiversity we need to reduce human demand on the planet. Bill Laurance, a research professor at Australia's James Cook University, and Paul Ehrlich, President of the Center for Conservation Biology at America's Stanford University, argue that we need to:

1. Slow the rate of human population growth;
2. Reduce overconsumption and overhunting;
3. Save remaining wilderness areas;
4. Expand and better protect our nature reserves;
5. Invest in conserving critically endangered species.[26]

There are simple measures we can take to contribute to the solution. **Support overseas aid and development organisations.** The single most significant way to reduce the rate of global population growth is to reduce poverty. There is a direct correlation between the number of children women have and the depth of poverty they experience. For example, in poorer communities the absence of social security payments for the aged often drives large family size for it enables households to spread the cost of caring for their elderly.

**Reduce meat consumption.** Approximately half the habitable land on earth is occupied by farming and 80% of farmland is dedicated to growing livestock or the grain used to feed livestock.[27] Given it is those who are affluent who have diets heavy in animal protein, the growth in the world's middleclass will increasing demand for meat. A way forward would be for those of us who are affluent to shift to diets that are less reliant on animal protein. This would see a greater proportion of land devoted to growing crops for food, which is far less demanding on the earth than devoting land to livestock production.

It is likely that the global population will reach 9-10 billion by 2050 and then stabilise or decline. Scientists have argued that to prevent further biodiversity loss and accommodate a global population of that size around 90% of humankind's diet must be from plant-based foods. In addition to this we will need to replace livestock such as cattle, goats and sheep, that have a high demand on the environment, with lower demand animals such as poultry and pigs, and farm them in more energy efficient ways.[28]

**Participate in advocacy campaigns** run by groups such as World Wide Fund for Nature that lobby governments to set policies that improve biodiversity. Details can be found on WWFs website.

## Eco-discipline: Consumption

Changing your shopping habits can be a powerful way to steward the earth. This week do the following:

1. Replace 1-2 meat based meals with plant based meals;
2. Explore the green earth guide at earthfirst.net.au to identify 5-10 earth-friendly changes you can make to your shopping.

………………………………………………………………………...........

Chapter 3

# A New Heaven and a New Earth

In 1987 my wife and I, newly married, honeymooned in the Whitsunday Islands, a glorious stretch of tropical islands that form a gateway to the Great Barrier Reef. We travelled to the outer reef aboard a large commercial tourist vessel. Once we arrived at the reef we donned snorkeling gear and jumped in. It was like leaping into joy. I had entered a breathtakingly beautiful world. Corals of red, yellow and purple stretched out across the ocean floor. I was surrounded by schools of beautifully adorned fish, from the graceful angelfish with its bands of yellow and black, to the rainbow colours of the parrotfish with its strange beak, to the brilliant orange and white stripes of the tiny clownfish nestling in a red sea anemone. I felt the excited wonderment of a small child.

Two and a half decades later Sandy and I celebrated our 25th anniversary in Borneo. We spent a night on Selingen Island, one of the few places on earth where, under the cover of darkness, sea turtles crawl from the water, heave themselves across the beach, and lay their eggs. In hushed silence we stood before one of these majestic creatures as it laid dozens of eggs in the nest it had dug. The next morning we witnessed hundreds of hatchlings crawl up from beneath the sand and, resembling wound up toys suddenly released, furiously rotate their flippers as they made a dash for the water. It's difficult to describe how profoundly moving it was to witness. It seemed that life itself was parading before us.

Yet according to the traditional understanding of salvation with which I grew up all this is of little worth. Our focus was not to be placed on things of the earth but on the things of heaven, for the centerpiece of history was the grand struggle for the destiny of the soul. The earth was merely the stage upon which this drama was played out, to be left behind as our souls found their eternal home in either the immaterial realm of heaven or the painful torments of hell. We were to be about the saving of souls and should avoid distraction by the things of the earth.

This type of thinking continues to influence many Christians. They remain committed to the notion that the "spiritual" (by which they mean the immaterial) must be prioritised over the physical, and the eternal over the temporary, and in doing so they make care of creation peripheral to faith. It is rarely, if ever, the subject of preaching, prayer, or action in their church, and they don't frame their discipleship with reference to the earth.

In the last two decades theologians such as Richard Middleton and NT Wright have helped us see salvation in an entirely different light[29], to recognise that the movement in the Bible is not from earth to heaven but from heaven to earth, that salvation does not consist of souls being released from their bodies for an eternity in heaven but of the resurrection of the body, so that redeemed people with redeemed hearts, minds and bodies, live in just, graceful and loving communities on a redeemed and restored earth. Far from merely being the stage upon which the drama of salvation is played out, creation is part of the drama. From start to finish the message of the Bible is that God is saving his entire creation.

# The Bookends of the Bible

The Bible opens with the creation of the world and closes with a vision of the world made new. Genesis 1 speaks of God calling the universe into being, first creating the physical structures of the universe (Days 1-3) and then populating them with creatures of the sea, air and land (Days 4-6). Human beings are not distinguished by the possession of a soul, but by their status as the image of God and their calling to rule the animals and subdue the earth. In other words, human beings are embodied beings, a point emphasised when the second chapter of Genesis tells us that "the Lord God formed man from the dust of the ground, and breathed into his nostrils the breath of life; and the man became a living being" (verse 7). The first human being, "the Adam", was created from the dust of the earth, which in Hebrew is "the Adamah". This play on words could be captured in English by saying God created the earthling from the dust of the earth. Having been formed from the dust, God animates the man by breathing into his nostrils. This does not reference the impartation of a soul but the imparting of life, something human beings share with the animals (Genesis 1:30; 6:17; 7:15, 22). From the very outset we were designed to be physical beings who found our home in the material creation.

It is this understanding that informs the biblical view of salvation. Far from imagining disembodied spirits floating through an immaterial realm, the book which concludes the bible, the book of Revelation, sees the future as a new heavens and earth populated by embodied beings enjoying life as it was always intended to be.

In Revelation chapters 1-3 Christ addresses the churches of Asia Minor, but in chapter 4 there is an arresting change of scene in which John is transported to the throne room of God. Winged creatures fly around the throne proclaiming God's holiness; peals of thunder and flashes of lightning issue from the throne; and twenty-four elders dressed in white and wearing gold crowns sit on smaller thrones worshipping God. As John stares at the throne he sees a scroll in the hand of God. The context suggests the scroll contains God's plan for the future of the universe. It is sealed with seven wax seals. Once those seals are broken the glorious future God intends can be unfurled.

It dawns on John that there is no one who is able to break the seals and open the scroll, and he breaks down into heaving sobs. He has seen the brutality of Rome, this empire that exploited the poor with its greedy acquisition of their resources; crushed dissent and murdered his Lord. If no one can open the scroll then the future will be no more than a rerun of the present. The future will be nothing but Rome and its equally destructive successors.

John's anguish is relieved when he learns that there is someone who can open the scroll, the crucified and risen Christ. The rest of the book recounts the momentous events that take place as each wax seal is broken, until finally the forces of evil are routed. The violent, terrorising empire is overthrown and the new world mapped out in the scroll becomes reality. It is "a new heaven and a new earth" where

> *the home of God is among mortals. He will dwell with them; they will be his peoples, and God himself will be with them; he will wipe every tear from their eyes. Death will be no more; mourning and crying and pain will be no more, for the first things have passed away.* Revelation 21:3–4

The capital of this new world is "the Holy City, the new Jerusalem". It stands in stark contrast to its greedy, violent, and oppressive predecessor, Babylon. Images from Eden and the prophetic hope for Jerusalem are fused. The tree of life from which humankind was barred after the sin of Adam and Eve now straddles the river of the water of life that flows through the city. It bears fruit and eating its leaves brings healing to the nations. The curses of Genesis 3 that made toil wearisome, childbirth dangerous, and put enmity between the snake and humankind, are lifted. By these devices John signals that the future God will create is the future imagined in the creation stories. It will not be an endless rerun of violent and oppressive regimes.

Of course, apocalyptic imagery was never intended to be a photographic image. It is filled with symbolism, so we should not hurriedly assume that John is doing anything other than affirming that salvation will result in a world where evil has ended and God reigns. Nonetheless, it is instructive that this framework of thinking is not that of humanity leaving earth behind and ascending to heaven, but rather heaven coming to earth and transforming it.

## The Prophetic Vision of Salvation

The Old Testament prophets speak similarly. They declare God's judgement upon the Israelites and the nations, called forth by the violence, injustice and exploitation that issue from idolatry. But beyond judgement they see restoration of Israel and the nations.

This vision is captured spectacularly in Isaiah 65:17-25. God declares his intention to create "a new heaven and a new earth" in which "Jerusalem will be a delight". Life on this new earth is painted in terms that would have made sense to the small scale agriculture community of Isaiah's time. Against their lived reality of dispossession, poverty, violence and exploitation, in God's new world people will live long, healthy and happy lives free from fear, violence and exploitation. Each household will be secure on its own plot of land and enjoy the fruit of its labour and the presence and blessing of God. Even the animals will cease preying on one another.

Daniel 7 describes the coming of salvation as the overthrow of oppressive and violent governments and the establishment of an eternal and universal kingdom marked by justice. The present is imagined in terms of four ferocious beasts that represent a succession of governments, each violently devouring all before them. The time comes when they are destroyed by God and a new leader is installed. This leader does not have the appearance of a beast, but of a human, signifying that his reign will correspond to God's intention for humankind. His kingdom will be just, compassionate and good. And it will be eternal.

Turn to Micah and the future is pictured as a time when the nations flock to the temple of Yahweh to learn his ways. Yahweh will

> *judge between many peoples,*
>
> *and shall arbitrate between strong nations far away;*
>
> *they shall beat their swords into ploughshares,*
>
> *and their spears into pruning-hooks;*

*nation shall not lift up sword against nation,*

*neither shall they learn war anymore;*

*but they shall all sit under their own vines and under their own fig trees,*

*and no one shall make them afraid* (4:3-4)

Isaiah, Daniel, Micah and the rest of the Old Testament prophets share a common vision of salvation. As we saw within the book of Revelation, this does not involve a flight from earth to heaven, but of heaven to earth, remaking the world into everything it was intended to be at creation.

# The Resurrection

In the New Testament the image of salvation is framed around the concept of resurrection.

In *Surprised By Hope* renowned theologian Tom Wright coined the phrase "life after life after death." He suggests that life after death is a two-stage affair. In the first stage we find ourselves apart from our bodies but in the presence of God. In the second stage we are given new bodies and live on a new earth.

Like most Christians of my era, I imagined only the first stage, that after death I would spend eternity as a disembodied spirit living with God in heaven. Tom Wright points out that this disembodied state is only temporary, for the ultimate goal is resurrection. The goal of salvation is the restoration of our selves, our communities, and our world to what God envisaged when he created – human beings with healthy bodies, loving hearts, and redeemed minds; living in communities marked by justice, love, grace and worship; nourished physically and emotionally by a functioning material environment.

The most extended discussion of the resurrection comes in 1 Corinthians 15, where the apostle Paul describes the risen Jesus as the "first fruits" of what will be the story of humanity. When Israelites farmed their land they would bring the first portion of the harvest to God in an offering of thanksgiving, knowing that the first fruits anticipated the entire harvest. In a similar way, says Paul, the resurrection of Christ anticipates what will happen to us all upon his return. If he was raised from the dead, so shall we be; if he was raised to life free from decay and death, so shall we be; if he was raised to a body suited to life in the Spirit, so shall we be.

As with the Old Testament prophets, salvation in the New Testament ultimately involves not a flight from earth to heaven, but heaven coming to earth and remaking it. In Philippians 3 we read

> *But our citizenship is in heaven, and it is from there that we are expecting a Saviour, the Lord Jesus Christ. He will transform the body of our humiliation so that it may be conformed to the body of his glory, by the power that also enables him to make all things subject to himself.*

Our citizenship in heaven does not mean our home is there but that our identity, our loyalty and our belonging are with Christ, who will come from heaven to earth and transform our bodies. In Romans 8 the apostle Paul expands this theme. Not only will individuals be raised to new life, so too will the entire creation:

> *I consider that the sufferings of this present time are not worth comparing with the glory about to be revealed to us. For the creation waits with eager longing for the revealing of the children of God; for the creation was subjected to futility, not of its own will but by the will of the one who subjected it, in hope that the creation itself will be set free from its bondage to decay and will obtain the freedom of the glory of the children of God. We know that the whole creation has been groaning in labor pains until now; and not only the creation, but we ourselves, who have the first fruits of the Spirit, groan inwardly while we wait for adoption, the redemption of our bodies. For in hope we were saved. Romans 8:18-24.*

Life was difficult for most people living in the first century. The bulk of the population lived in poverty, large numbers were enslaved, and many feared supernatural spirits. Cramped living conditions meant that disease would often spread like wildfire through communities, and without modern medical technology, would often prove fatal. To this reality the Christian gospel brought hope, but it was not hope of escape from the body and escape from this world, but hope for the re-creation of both. The pattern for the future would not be the release of the soul to return to the immaterial realm to which it belongs, as argued by many Greco-Roman religions, but rather, the resurrection of all things as foreshadowed by the resurrection of Jesus. The creation itself, the planet on which we live, will, argues Paul, be liberated from bondage to decay. Ever since humankind's first sin, creation has been marred, its capacity to be an abundant and hospitable environment for humankind and the animals diminished. The time will come however, when the earth will be restored to everything it was intended to be. And at the same time we will receive the "redemption of our bodies". Notice the text doesn't speak of the redemption of our souls, but our bodies. The whole person is to be saved, our consciousness, our emotions, our bodies.

Our ultimate destiny is to have transformed bodies, minds, emotions and will and to live in transformed communities on a transformed earth. Salvation is not about our souls being rescued from the creation, but the rescue of the creation itself, including human beings. It is not a temporary home upon which the true drama of history, the struggle for the human soul is played out. It is rather the place we belong and the place we will belong. The drama of history is vastly broader than the salvation of human individuals. It is nothing less than God's work to bring healing to the entire created order.

..............................................................................

# A New Creation or a Renewed Creation?

There is a strong tradition in the church that says the earth and everything in it will be destroyed and replaced with a brand new earth. This can then be used as an argument against care for the present planet.

First, whether or not God will destroy the present planet, the Bible is clear that God values our planet and its creatures. This alone should lead us to reject suggestions we should not care about creation.

Second, we ought to interpret with humility. I saw a movie a few years ago in which a young man explained colour to his blind friend. He placed a rock in the oven, pulled it out and handed it to her. While she was juggling the hot rock the young man said "that's red. It's hot and fiery". He then took a rock out of the fridge and handed it to her. "That's blue. It's cool and refreshing." The only way the young man could explain colour to someone who had never seen it was to compare colour to something she could understand. Is it the same with biblical descriptions of salvation? Will salvation transcend anything we know but is a reality that is best compared to living in a perfected world?

Third, the New Testament pattern for the future is resurrection, which involves both continuity and discontinuity with the present. Jesus's resurrection body was his human body imbued with new qualities. For example, it was no longer subject to ageing, decay, disease, or death; he was able to pass through walls; his body was fit for life in the Spirit (see 1 Corinthians 15:35-58). If resurrection of Christ involved continuity and discontinuity with this life, it makes sense that the same will be true of the restoration of creation.

Fourth, 2 Peter 3:9-10, the text most commonly cited when suggesting God will destroy the earth, says

> *The Lord is not slow about his promise, as some think of slowness, but is patient with you, not wanting any to perish, but all to come to repentance. But the day of the Lord will come like a thief, and then the heavens will pass away with a loud noise, and the elements will be dissolved with fire, and the earth and everything that is done on it will be disclosed.*

The passage can be interpreted and thus translated in a number of ways. The NRSV translation given above follows the argument shared by Richard Baulkham, who notes that the passage employs apocalyptic thought forms to describe the exposure of humankind to the full glare of God's judgement.[30] The passage imagines humanity to be hidden by the "elements", spiritual and material realities that stand between God and humankind. It is these elements rather than the earth that are dissolved, leaving the earth's inhabitants exposed to God, with nowhere to hide.

# Redeeming Creation

It is time for us to recover the breadth of the biblical vision of salvation, to let go of the hubris that says we humans are the only beings that matter, and to jettison the notion that our eternal destiny is an immaterial heaven.

When we stand amazed before a sunset and perceive in it the glory of God, we recognise the ways God currently reigns. When we see the brokenness of creation, whether that be the destructive force of an earthquake, the debilitating power of disease, or the unwelcome intrusion of death, and imagine a future where there is no more death, mourning, crying or pain, we anticipate the ways God will one day reign. And in the meantime, we look for the evidence of God's reign in the present, whether it be through a person coming to faith, a wounded spirit finding comfort, a community where relationships have broken down finding reconciliation, or through the reversal of the degrading of the environment.

There is no room in this age of ecological crisis for us to sing "this world is not my home". The sure and certain testimony of the Bible is that the world is our home and that a recreated earth will be our home for eternity. When we work for the flourishing of the creation we are doing nothing less than joining God in his work of establishing his reign.

# Eco-concern: Climate Change

The earth is surrounded by a layer of gases such as carbon dioxide and water vapour that trap heat from the sun, leaving the earth at a temperature where life as we know it is possible. Natural cycles move large amounts of carbon dioxide between the atmosphere, the land and the oceans. For example, plants absorb carbon dioxide when they photosynthesise but release it into the atmosphere when they decompose; where the ocean surface is cool it absorbs carbon dioxide from the air but warmer parts of the ocean release carbon dioxide.

When we started burning fossil fuels such as coal and oil we took carbon that had been stored underground for millions of years and released it into the atmosphere as carbon dioxide. Oceans and plants absorbed some of this carbon, but enough of it has stayed in the atmosphere to increase the concentration of carbon dioxide by almost half (from 270 parts per million to around 400 parts per million). As a result, more heat is being trapped in our atmosphere, changing the world's climate.

On a business-as-usual scenario warming will likely be 2.6°-4.8°C higher by 2100 than at the start of this century. The Intergovernmental Panel on Climate Change (IPCC) states that

> *Without additional mitigation efforts beyond those in place today, and even with adaptation, warming by the*

*end of the 21st century will lead to high to very high risk of severe, widespread and irreversible impacts globally.*[31]

Climate change will amplify existing risks to wellbeing and create new ones. For example, storms will become more frequent and more intense; heatwaves will also be more frequent and last longer. In a world where 1 billion people are already hungry and the global population is growing, it is predicted that climate change will undermine food security. Warming oceans will see a redistribution of fish species, leaving many of the world's poor who currently depend upon fishing with even less. In many of the world's poorest countries wheat, rice and maize production will be negatively impacted. If the temperature rises above 4° the impacts on global food security will be great.

The IPCC's Fifth Assessment Report identifies the key risks for each region of the world. In each scenario, the impacts are substantially worse at 4° of warming than at 2°:

| | |
|---|---|
| **AFRICA** | Reductions in the availability of fresh water; large-scale reductions in crop productivity, livelihoods and food security; and the spread of vector and waterborne diseases. |
| **ASIA** | increased flood damage; increases in deaths from heatwaves; and increased drought-related water and food |

| | |
|---|---|
| | shortages. |
| **AUSTRALASIA** | damage to coral reefs and increased flood and storm damage. |
| **EUROPE** | increased damages from river and costal floods; increased water restrictions; increased damages from extreme heatwaves and wildfires. |
| **NORTH AMERICA** | increased damages from wildfires; deaths from heatwaves; increased damages from river and costal floods; |
| **CENTRAL & SOUTH AMERICA** | Reduced water availability, increased flooding and landslides; reduced food production and quality; spread of water-borne diseases. |

The Fifth Assessment Report modelled different scenarios and rated their likelihood of keeping temperature rises below 2°C. To give us a reasonable chance, by 2050 the world must reduce its greenhouse gas emissions by 41-72% compared to 2010 and by 2100 the reductions must reach 78-118%. It should be noted however that most of the models that yield this outcome assume we will go past the level of emissions required to stay below 2° but develop technologies that allow us to extract greenhouse gases from the atmosphere. Yet it is questionable whether these technologies will be viable, which means we will need to hit the reduction targets much earlier.

Our response to global warming must be twofold. First, we will need to adapt. The amount of gases already emitted mean that some warming is now unavoidable, and given the inability of the world's leaders to take sufficiently decisive action, the rises in temperature could be large. Adaption might mean farmers changing the mix of crops they grow; early warning systems to alert people when extreme weather events are imminent; and building seawalls to protect against rising sea levels.

Second, we must take action to limit future warming of the planet. This requires significant changes to how we produce, use and consume energy, and to how we practice agriculture. For example, electricity can be produced in ways that emit much fewer greenhouse gases than burning coal. These include wind farms, solar panels, and a range of other technologies that are still under development or to be developed. In the transport area mass-transit infrastructure and urban redevelopment can be pursued, along with improvements to the efficiency of motor vehicles. Buildings can be constructed in ways that use less energy. A shift away from heavy dependence upon meat from large animals to meat from smaller animals and higher amounts of grains would allow us to replant forests and possibly turn agriculture from a source of carbon emissions into a net carbon sink.[32]

Achieving these changes will require governments to

create incentives that signal to business and consumers the benefits of climate friendly production and consumption. Incentives can be created through things such as taxes upon products that are not climate friendly, which in turn makes the climate friendly product more competitive; and investment in research and development.

If we start early, the Fifth Assessment Report estimates the costs to economic growth will be around 0.04% to 0.14% per year. Given consumption is expected to grow between 1.6% and 3% each year, dealing with climate change now means that instead of growing 1.6-3% richer each year, the world would grow 1.46-2.96% richer each year.

## Eco-discipline: Footprint

Find the global footprint page at wwf.org.au and use the calculator to estimate your environmental footprint. Implement at least two of the recommendations for reducing your footprint.

Chapter 4.

# The Greatest Commandments

In 1986 the archaeological world was aflame with the news that the fully intact hull of a first century fishing boat had been uncovered in the mud of the Sea of Galilee. James, John & Peter would have fished from a boat just like this when Jesus called them to be his followers. It was a stunning discovery.

1986 was also the year that construction commenced on the "Moonzund" class of fishing super-trawler, a vessel that would have been unimaginable to those first century fishermen who plied their trade on the Sea of Galilee. The Jesus-boat was just 8.2 metres long, the super-trawler 120 metres. The Jesus-boat traversed the Sea of Galilee, the super-trawler traverses oceans. The fishermen in the Jesus-boat depended upon their eyes to locate fish, the super-trawler uses sophisticated sonar and satellite technologies. The Jesus boat could haul a modest amount of fish from the waters of the Sea of Galilee, but in a single day the super-trawler can catch and process 220 tonnes of fish.

These two boats sum up the changing relationship of humanity to creation. From the time of the Jesus-boat to the time of the super-trawler, human beings have called upon the resources of the planet to meet their needs. We have always cleared land, grown crops, fished the seas, built homes, domesticated animals, and created civilisations. In the process we changed the environment. But in the era of the super-trawler we are doing so on a scale exponentially greater than at any other point in history.

At the time of the Jesus-boat the global population was less than 200 million. In the era of the super-trawler it is 7 billion and expected to grow to 10 billion by 2050. All things being equal, this means humankind is demanding thirty-five times more from the planet than at the time of Jesus. All things are not, however, equal for not only has the total number of people calling upon the earth's resources increased, the era of the super-trawler has also seen a massive increase in the per person demand on the earth. The Industrial Revolution unleashed a period of astonishing growth in humankind's capacity to manipulate the planet. It allowed us to construct super-trawlers powered by massive diesel engines, guided by satellites and sophisticated electronics, that drag massive mechanised nets that scoop up tonnes of fish at a time. It gave us trains, planes and automobiles; air conditioners and microwaves; MRIs and X-Rays; skyscrapers and space-stations. The improvements in our quality-of-life have been extraordinary, but so has the cost to the planet. As we noted in previous chapters, our climate is changing in ways that are harmful and biodiversity is plummeting.

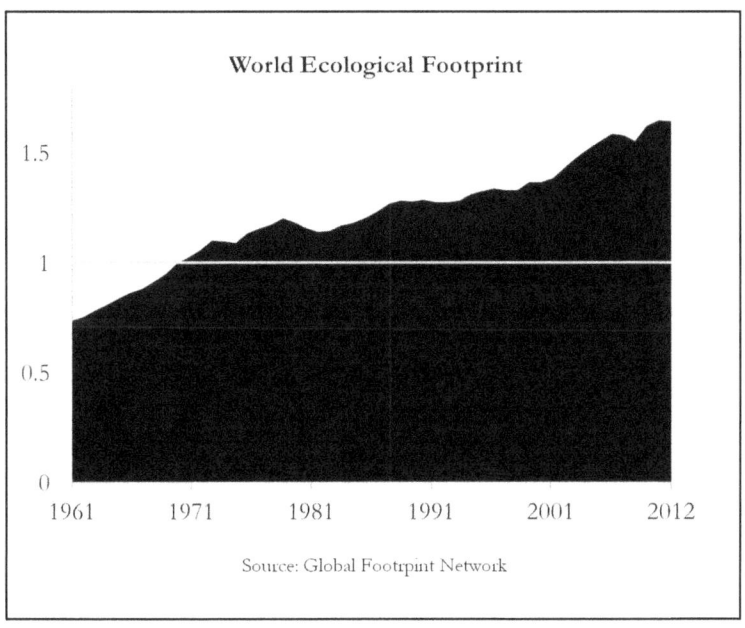

The global footprint chart is perhaps the most vivid way to conceptualise this. Produced by a group of scientists who make up the Global Footprint Network, the chart shows the area of land (measured in number of planet Earths) that would be required to sustainably produce the food, water, fuel, timber, etc that people use each year. Before 1970 less than one planet Earth was needed to sustainably produce what people consume but today it would take one and a half planets—which is rather more planets than we have at our disposal.

...................................................................................

# Following Jesus in the Age of the Super-Trawler

What does it mean to be a follower of Jesus in this age of the super-trawler? Some Christians notice that Jesus spoke barely a word about caring for the environment. He did not say, "Love the Lord your God, love your neighbour and love the earth." When he spoke about the way we are to live his emphasis was clear:

> *"You shall love the Lord your God with all your heart, and with all your soul, and with all your mind." This is the greatest and first commandment. And a second is like it: "You shall love your neighbour as yourself." On these two commandments hang all the law and the prophets.'*

Jesus may not have mentioned the environment, but in the era of the super trawler loving our neighbour and loving God have inescapable ecological dimensions. How we are treating the planet has dramatic implications for the well-being of our fellow human beings. The World Health Organisation points out that climate change means heatwaves, floods and storms are becoming more frequent and more intense; that temperature sensitive diseases are spreading into places they have never been experienced before; and that in many parts of the world crop yields are negatively impacted. Even with continued global economic growth, WHO estimates that climate change will result in 250,000 additional deaths per year between 2030 and 2050: 38,000 due to heat exposure in elderly people, 48,000 due to diarrhoea, 60,000 due to malaria, and 95,000 due to childhood undernutrition.[33]

In the highlands of Kenya, malaria, which is one of the greatest killers of children under the age of five, is appearing in places that had previously been free of it. It is believed the causes of this might include global warming (the increase in temperature in the Highlands may only be slight, but it is enough to allow the mosquitoes that bear the malaria virus to survive at altitudes they previously could not) and changed land use (which sees more water puddles create more breeding grounds for mosquitoes).[34]

In the years leading up to the 2004/5 tsunami, stands of mangroves were removed from the Thai coastline to make way for prawn farms. When the tsunami struck, those communities who had left their mangroves in place saw far less destruction than those who had removed their mangroves, for mangroves serve to dampen storm surge.[35]

These are just three examples of how our degradation of the environment is impacting negatively upon our fellow human beings.

In the era of the Jesus-boat loving my neighbour meant responding with generosity and grace to the people I encountered as I went about my daily business. It was to show hospitality to the stranger who entered my village; to share my food and harvest with those in my village who were landless; to care for neighbours who were sick. In the era of the super-trawler loving my neighbour continues to mean these things, but also takes us beyond them. If our demand upon the planet is harming people, particularly those who are poor, and diminishing the capacity of the earth to provide for future generations, surely love demands change in our behaviour?

Similarly, in the era of the Jesus-boat, loving God means loving the things God loves, and this includes the world he made. In chapter 1 we observed the great love God has for all he has made and the joy God derives from his creation. How then can we glibly excuse our destruction of the creatures and places God loves?

# Living with Limits

The core problem is that we are over-consuming the resources of the planet. Moreover, the wealthier we are the more we consume. The 2012 ecological footprint of those in high income countries was 6.2 global hectares per person, compared to 2.3 global hectares per person for those in middle income countries and just one global hectare per person in low income countries.[36]

The desire to accumulate is nothing new. The writer to Ecclesiastes observed that those who get more are never satisfied (5:10). Jesus warned us to be on the guard against greed, insisting that life does not consist in the abundance of our possessions (Luke 12:15). The problem was not that there was something inherently wrong about enjoying the good things of God's earth; it was that this worked against communities in which everybody had sufficient.

Like most premodern economies, the economy of ancient Israel was built around the notion of "limited goods". Israel, with the exception of the tribe of Levi, was a nation of small-scale farmers. Each household was given land on which they would grow their own food and provide for their own needs. If a person lost their land they lost the means to sustain themselves and their household. To guard against this, the Old Testament law contained a number of provisions that helped people appreciate the things they had while at the same time limiting their capacity to acquire their neighbour's land.

Throughout the year a number of festivals were held in which the Israelites celebrated God's provision (Leviticus 23). The feast of firstfruits was held at the beginning of each harvest season. A sheaf from the first grain harvested would be brought to God in a ceremony of thanksgiving, reminding the worshipper that God had given them a fruitful and abundant land (Leviticus 23:9-14). The tithe festival saw Israelite households spending 10% of their annual income on a weeklong celebration in which they remembered God's goodness to them (Deuteronomy 14:24-

29).

Alongside these rituals of thanksgiving and celebration, were systems designed to restrain greed and cultivate neighbourliness. Take the Old Testament concept of Sabbath. The Israelites celebrated a day-long Sabbath every week, during which all people and farm animals were to be given a day of rest from their labour. Walter Brueggeman writes that in the weekly Sabbath the Israelites

> *are invited to awareness that life does not consist in frantic production and consumption that reduces everyone else to threat or competitor. And as the work stoppage permits a waning of anxiety, so energy is redeployed to the neighbourhood. The odd insistence of the God of Sinai is to counter anxious productivity with committed neighbourliness. The latter practice does not produce so much; but it creates an environment of security and respect and dignity that redefines the human project.*[37]

In addition to the weekly Sabbath, a year-long sabbath was held every seven years, during which the land was given rest from harvesting and debts were forgiven. Every 50 years a super Sabbath, the Jubilee, was held during which all land was returned to the families to whom it had originally been given. This recalibrated the economy back to an equal standing for all.

The rise of capitalism and its capacity to create wealth liberated humankind from the notion that for one person to have more someone else had to have less, and has seen hundreds of millions of people lifted out of poverty. It also created the illusion that having more never involves loss to somebody else. Sometimes it does, and this is particularly the case with regards to our use of the earth. God has given us a planet with the capacity to renew itself, but that is not an unlimited capacity. The simple reality is that we must change our production and consumption habits so that the resources of the planet are available to all living creatures both now into the future.

We will do well to learn the lessons of festival and Sabbath, to celebrate the astonishing and satisfying sufficiency of the planet, and to create systems that promote neighbourliness and curtail greed.

We will not achieve the required change by tinkering at the edges of our behaviour. Living sustainably will require substantial changes in our patterns of production and consumption. Take energy as an example. To prevent highly dangerous levels of climate change, we need to get our emissions to a net level of zero by around 2050. This can only be achieved by addressing consumption and production. On one hand, we can reduce our consumption of energy. For example, we can make our buildings and motor vehicles more energy efficient; make greater use of public transport; choose to put on warm clothing rather than turn up the air conditioning. However, to get to zero net emissions, we also that we need to make changes to how we produce energy. We could switch electricity production away from burning of fossil fuels towards renewable sources such as wind, solar, and thermal.

Our action must be personal, political and prayerful. Each of us must personally take responsibility to live sustainably, to find ways to reduce our demand upon the earth. For example, we can resist the throwaway nature of modern culture and elect to repair and reuse things rather than simply replacing them; we can choose products that are produced in an environmentally friendly fashion; we can reduce our energy use or swap our energy supplies over to renewable resources.

Personal change alone will not, however, get us to the point we need. For the world to successfully meet the challenges it faces, collective action is required. We need governments and corporations to implement policies that lead to sustainable living. As citizens who elect those governments and consumers who purchase products services we are able to use our voices to influence than to change.

Finally, we ought to be prayerful. Prayer reminds us that God is the Creator of the world and is committed to its salvation. It is an opportunity for humble repentance and an occasion for hope.

………………………………………………………...............

# Eco-concern: Nitrogen & Acidification

## The nitrogen cycle

All living things depend upon nitrogen for their growth. The nitrogen cycle ensures that adequate supplies of nitrogen flow where needed. Nitrogen is extracted from the air by plants, transferred to the animal population when they consume plants or consume animals that have consumed plants, passed into the soil as animals decompose and from there is passed back into the air.

In the 1800s scientists discovered how to extract nitrogen from the air and use it to create fertilisers. This has allowed us to dramatically increase crop yields around the world, but we are now producing so much nitrogen that it is leeching off land and into rivers and oceans where it fuels the growth of algal blooms that suck oxygen from the water and create massive dead zones.

## Acidification of the oceans

A substantial portion of the increases in carbon dioxide emissions that have occurred since the Industrial Revolution have been absorbed by the oceans, which has caused them to become more acidic. This has a number of serious impacts. Coral reefs, for example, are a source of fish for many communities around the world and play an important role in protecting shorelines from storm surge. Many coral polyps build their outer skeletons by secreting calcium carbonate but as the oceans become more acidic it is harder for them to do this. If acidification continues the stage will eventually be reached were ocean waves erode coral reefs faster than the polyps can build them.

## Eco-discipline: Advocate

If humankind is to live within the ecological limits of the planet we need to act personally and politically. That is, we each need to start incorporating eco-friendly changes into our lifestyles and we need changes to our social, economic, and political systems. Write a letter to your local Member of Parliament describing what you have learned during this series, what action you are personally undertaking to make change, and urging your local MP to ensure Australia takes strong action on pressing environmental issues.

For more specific details of what you might ask your MP visit micahaustralia.org or ajustcause.com.au.

..................................................................................................

# Discussion Guide

These four Bible studies are designed for use by small groups. They provide have an opportunity for groups to explore the Scriptures to discover what it means for us to live as God's people in God's world.

Each study has three sections:

1. opening up the issue: a discussion question that raises the issue that will be the focus of the study;
2. opening up the Bible: two or three questions that invite you to consider what the Bible says about the issue;
3. opening up our lives: a question that invites discussion of how you can implement what you have learned in your living and in your church and an eco-discipline to implement before the next study.

# Study 1.
# The Earth is the Lord's

Why does our world exist? Christians affirm that God created the universe, did so with purpose, and that we should value the world in a way that respects that purpose. But what was that purpose?

A common argument through history has been that the world was created for humankind. On this reckoning God's goal in creation was to have a relationship with humankind. It is we who are the point of creation, we who are the focus of God's love, and everything that God created was designed to serve this relationship.

But what if there is more to creation than this? What if it wasn't all made for us? What if God's love and purposes extend to all living creatures? How would this change the way we value and treat the planet and its life?

## Opening Up the Issue

1. St Francis of Assisi wrote a famous prayer called the Canticle of Creation. Take time as a group to read it aloud. How comfortable do you feel praying this prayer? Is the language of "brother sun" and "sister wind" helpful or off-putting? Why do you think this is?

............................................................................

## Canticle of Creation (first part)

*O Most High, all-powerful, good Lord God,*
*to you belong praise, glory, honour and all blessing.*

*Be praised, my Lord, for all your creation*
*and especially for our Brother Sun,*
*who brings us the day and the light;*
*he is strong and shines magnificently.*
*O Lord, we think of you when we look at him.*

*Be praised, my Lord, for Sister Moon,*
*and for the stars which you have set shining and lovely*
*in the heavens.*

*Be praised, my Lord, for our Brothers Wind and Air*
*and every kind of weather by which you, Lord,*
*uphold life in all your creatures.*

*Be praised, my Lord, for Sister Water,*
*who is very useful to us,*
*and humble and precious and pure.*

*Be praised, my Lord, for Brother Fire,*
*through whom you give us light in the darkness:*
*he is bright and lively and strong.*

*Be praised, my Lord,*
*for Sister Earth, our Mother,*
*who nourishes us and sustains us,*
*bringing forth fruits and vegetables of many kinds*
*and flowers of many colours.*

..............................................................................

# Opening Up the Bible

2. Genesis 1 speaks of God creating the world over six days and resting on the seventh. Throughout history interpreters commonly suggested that the climax of the story is the creation of humankind on day six. On this reading everything is created with humankind in mind and is designed to serve the interests of humankind. A number of scholars argue that this is mistaken and that the climax of the story is the rest of God on day seven. On this reading everything is created to reflect the glory of God and to serve the interests of God. Old Testament scholar John Walton comments that

*In the traditional view...day seven is mystifying. It appears to be nothing more than an afterthought with theological concerns about Israelites observing the Sabbath – an appendix, a postscript, a tack on.*

*In contrast, a reader from the ancient world would know immediately what was going on and recognise the role of day seven. Without hesitation the ancient reader would conclude that this is a temple text and that day seven is the most important of the seven days.*

*... How could reactions be so different? The difference is the piece of information that everyone knew in the ancient world and to which most modern readers are totally oblivious: divinity rests in a temple, and only in a temple.*

*...The most central truth to the creation account is that this*

*world is a place for God's presence.*
John Walton, *The Lost World of Genesis 1*

What difference do these two readings make to the way you view the creation, and to our relationship to it and to God? Which reading makes most sense to you?

3. At the heart of the Christian faith is the affirmation that God loves us. A number of biblical texts also speak of God's love for all living creatures - e.g. Psalm 104; Matthew 6:17-35. What difference should this make to the way we view and value the world and its creatures?

## Opening Up Our Lives

4. "For too long Christians have treated the earth and its creatures as irrelevant to Christian spirituality. If all creation is designed to reflect the glory and the presence of God, we should allow it to turn our hearts and our minds towards God. And if all creation is the object of God's love and care, it should be the object of our love and care." Do you agree? If so, how might we build a God-centred valuing of the creation into our living?

5. Eco discipline to implement this week: Take time each day to focus upon a particular part of creation – it could be a sunrise, a tree, or a pet. Reflect upon the ways this

part of creation points you to God, brings joy to God, and how you should value it.

. . . . . . . . . . . . . . . . . . . . . . . . . . . . . . . . . . . . . . . . . . . . . . . . . . . . . . . . . . . . . . . . . . . . . . ...........

# Study 2.
# Let Them Have Dominion

One of the distinguishing features of humankind is our drive to live meaningfully. We don't want to simply exist, we want our lives to matter. Around the time of the Renaissance (14th-17th century Europe) the idea emerged that to be human was to dominate the planet, to use the technologies that were emerging to bend it to our will. Before this we had seen the earth as a resource for our benefit, but now we saw a mandate to develop and conquer it.

Bible scholars started to interpret the image of God to mean we were given the power to create something out of the earth. The commands to rule over the animals and to subdue the planet were read as God's mandate that they serve human needs. But what if this interpretation has actually missed the point of Genesis 1? Could it be that our purpose as human beings is not simply to use creation but to care for it?

## Opening up the Issue

1. Rick Warren's *The Purpose Driven Life* was one of the most popular Christian books of past two decades. In this book Rick Warren suggests that God has five purposes

………………………………………………………………............

for our lives: to bring pleasure to God; to belong to God's family; to become like Christ; to serve God; to engage in mission to the world. The book helps the reader to explore each of these area, but at no point does the book discuss God's purpose for our lives in relationship to the earth. Do you think God has a purpose for us in relationship to the earth and its living creatures? If so, what is it?

## Opening Up the Bible

2. The creation stories are important texts in considering who we are and why we're here. Genesis 1 commissions humankind to rule over the animals and subdue the earth. This is at the core of what it is to be human, but what do these commands mean? Given we are to subdue the earth and rule the animals as God's representatives (that is, those made in the image of God) we will best understand their meaning by examining how God subdues and rules.

   a. Psalm 104 is a reflection on God's relationship to the earth and its creatures. What does this psalm suggest about the way God brings the earth under control and the ends for which God does this? What does this suggest about our calling to "subdue the earth"?

………………………………………………………………………………..............

b. Throughout the biblical eras rulers used their power to advance their own position and greatness. The Bible expects that rulers do the opposite, that they serve the interests of those they rule (e.g. Proverbs 31:1-9; Matthew 20:25-26). How do you see this concept reflected in God's rule of the creatures in Psalm 104? What would mean to apply it to our "rule over" the living creatures?

## Opening Up Our Lives

3. "When Christians speak of finding God purpose for their lives this must include the recognition that human beings were created to be the caretakers of God's planet. We are called to manage the earth and its resources in such a way that all living creatures thrive." Do you agree? Why/why not? How do you think humankind is doing? What are some things you and your church could do to live out your calling toward the earth & its creatures?

4. Eco-discipline to implement this week: Explore the green earth guide at earthfirst.net.au and identify 5-10 changes you can make to your shopping that are earth friendly.

………………………………………………………………...............

# Study 3.
# A New Heavens and Earth

One of the great tensions for Christians in their relationship to the planet and its creatures is our conviction that we will one day leave this earth and our bodies behind to spend an eternity with God in heaven. Why then would we invest ourselves in the planet and its creatures? They will pass away, but our spirit will live on. Should we not invest ourselves in matters of eternity and the spiritual?

That might be a logical conclusion, but in recent years a number of biblical scholars have pointed out that it is based upon a false premise. The idea that our true self is a soul trapped inside a body from which it is released at death comes to us from ancient Greek philosophies. The bible, however. grounds its thinking in resurrection. Just as Jesus was raised from death to life in a resurrected body, so too will we be, and we will live on a planet that is redeemed. The biblical image of the future is one in which we have resurrected bodies, live in whole and healed communities, on a very material planet that is abundant and hospitable.

NT Wright speaks of this as "life after life after death". By this he means that after death we will find ourselves in the presence of God in a disembodied state, but that this is only temporary, for the time will come when God will restore everything.

……………………………………………………………..............

## Opening Up the Issue

1. If you were to paint a picture of the popular view of heaven, what would it look like? Does this reflect your understanding of the future?

## Opening Up the Bible

2. Read Isaiah 65:17-25. This is typical of the prophetic vision for the future. If Isaiah's vision was painted, how would it be different from the piece of art you may have imagined in answer to question 1.

3. The New Testament writers consider the resurrection of Jesus to be the model for the future. How does this model apply to individuals and the entire created order in Romans 8:18-25? What does it suggest about the future of creation?

## Opening Up Our Lives

4. "For way too long we have had a limited vision of salvation, thinking that it was just about us and God and entry into heaven. The biblical vision is that God is saving the entire creation. If God is committed to saving the entire creation, we witness to this when we are concerned with combating that which destroys God's

good earth and working for its healthy functioning." Do you agree? Why/why not? How might you and your church give practical expression to this?

5. Eco-discipline to implement this week: Find the global footprint page at wwf.org.au and use the calculator to estimate your environmental footprint. Implement at least two of the recommendations for reducing your footprint.

. . . . . . . . . . . . . . . . . . . . . . . . . . . . . . . . . . . . . . . . . . . . . . . . . . . . . . . . . . . . . . . . . . . . . . . . . ..............

# Study 4.
# The Greatest Commandments

The world has changed dramatically since the time of Jesus. The global population has grown from less than 200 million to 7 billion and is on track to peak at 10 billion in 2050. This has been accompanied by an explosion in technological capacity that is environmentally intensive and the rise of the consumer society in which it is expected that we will keep growing acquiring more. All this means humankind is placing great demands on the planet, so much so that we are now altering the fundamental ecological systems upon which life depends.

Since the late 1960's we have been using the resources of the earth faster than they renew and ecological systems are starting to break down. Between 1970 and 2012 animal populations across the planet declined by 58% and animal species are becoming extinct at 1000 times the rate they would were it not for human interference. Our oceans are acidifying as they absorb the carbon dioxide we produce, resulting in the bleaching of coral reefs and the possible collapse of the oceanic food chain. Greenhouse gas emissions have been rising at such a rate that we are well on track to average global temperature increases of 3-4° by the end of the century. Extreme weather events such as storms, floods, and heat waves are becoming more intense and more frequent; sea levels are rising; and diseases are spreading to places they have not been found before. The World Health Organisation estimates that climate change will result in 250,000 additional deaths per year between 2030 and 2050.

What does it mean to be a follower of Jesus in a time such as this?

## Opening Up the Issue

1. Jesus told us to love God and love our neighbor, but he never told us to love the earth. Does this mean Christians should not be concerned about the state of the environment?

## Opening Up the Bible

2. The land to which God brought Israel after rescuing them from slavery in Egypt was described as "flowing with milk and honey". Life was not to be miserable and oppressive like it had been in Egypt. Israel's was to be a society in which every person enjoyed sufficiency. Such a society would only come into existence if people placed constraints around their desire to keep on acquiring more. Consider the Sabbaths of Israel: the Sabbath day (Exodus 20:8-11); the Sabbath year (Exodus 23:10-11; Deuteronomy 15:1-11); and the Sabbath of Jubilee (Leviticus 25: 8-24). In each instance how was the drive to acquire more at the expense of others contained in favour of a system that ensured everybody enjoyed the

fruitfulness of the earth? Do you think this same principle can be applied to our relationship with the earth today? What might modern ecological and social Sabbaths look like?

3. Jesus taught that the heart of discipleship is to love God with all our heart, soul, mind and strength, and to love our neighbour as ourselves. How can our engagement with creation be considered an act of love for God and love for others?

## Opening Up our Lives

4. "One of the most urgent needs facing humankind today is the ability to live within boundaries. We have to recognise that the planet is finite. It is not a limitless resource." Do you agree/disagree? Why/why not?

5. Eco-discipline for this week: if humankind is to live within the ecological limits of the planet we need to make significant changes to our consumption habits and to how we produce the resources we require. For example, we could reduce our consumption of meat; set aside more areas as nature reserves; and replace energy produced from fossil fuels with energy produced from renewable resources such as wind, solar and thermal.

..................................................................................

Action to this end needs to be both personal and political. That is we each need to start incorporating eco-friendly changes into our lifestyles and we need changes to our social, economic, and political systems. Write a letter to your local Member of Parliament (MP) describing what you have learned during this series, what action you are personally undertaking to make change, and urging your local MP to ensure Australia takes strong action on pressing environmental issues. (For more specific details of what you might ask your MP visit micahaustralia.org)

..................................................................................................

# End Notes

[1] Victoria Braithwaite, *Do Fish Feel Pain?* (Oxford University Press, 2010);
[2] Origen, *Contra Celsus*, 268. Translated by Frederick Crombie. From *Ante-Nicene Fathers*, Vol. 4. Edited by Alexander Roberts, James Donaldson, and A. Cleveland Coxe. (Buffalo, NY: Christian Literature Publishing Co., 1885.) Revised and edited for New Advent by Kevin Knight. http://www.newadvent.org/fathers/0416.htm.
[3] John Calvin, *Commentaries on Genesis*, Vol 1, Translated by the Rev. John King, Christian Classics Ethereal Library, Grand Rapids
[4] Gordon Wenham, *Genesis 1-15*, Word Biblical Commentary (Word, 1987) page 38
[5] See Richard Bauckham, "Dominion Interpreted - A Historical Account" in Bauckham, *Living with Other Creatures. Green Exegesis and Theology* (Paternoster 2012) pp 14-62
[6] Richard Bauckham, "The Human Place in Creation - A Biblical Overview" in Bauckham, *Living with Other Creatures*. p5
[7] John Walton, *The Lost World of Genesis One. Ancient Cosmology and the Genesis Debate*, (IVP Academic, 2009), 82-84
[8] Leslie Allen, *Psalms 101-150*, Word Biblical Commentary Series, Vol 21 (Word, 1983) p316
[9] Australian Bureau of Statistics 7215.0 – Livestock Products Australia
[10] Animal Health Alliance Australia, "Pet Ownership In Australia" (2013)
[11] RSPCA The Five Freedoms. http://kb.rspca.org.au/Five-freedoms-for-animals_318.pdf
[12] Rick Warren, *The Purpose Driven Life. What on Earth am I Here for?* (Zondervan 2011)
[13] Warren, *Purpose Driven Life*, p281
[14] Norman Habel, "Geophany. The Earth Story in Genesis 1" in Havel & Wurst (eds), *The Earth Story in Genesis* (Sheffield Acadmeic Press, 2000)
[15] J Richard Middleton, *The Liberating Image. The Imago Dei in Genesis 1* (Brazos Press, 2005)
[16] Gordon Wenham, *Genesis 1-15*, p31
[17] Nahum Sarna, *Understanding Genesis* (Schocken Books, 1966) p21
[18] I am indebted to private correspondence with Dr John Olley for this insight.
[19] WWF, Living Planet Report 2016. Risk and Resilience in a New Era (WWF International, 2016)
[20] WWF, *Living Planet Report 2016*.
[21] Sean L. Maxwell, Richard A. Fuller, Thomas M. Brooks, James E. M. Watson, "Biodiversity: The ravages of guns, nets and bulldozers" in *Nature news* (Nature

Publishing Group, 2016)
[22] Maxwell, et al, "Biodiversity"
[23] Australian Museum, "What's Happening to Australia's Biodiversity?" http://australianmuseum.net.au/whats-happening-to-australias-biodiversity
[24] Laurance and Ehrlich, "Radical overhaul needed to halt Earth's sixth great extinction event" The Conversation Website, November 9, 2016. https://theconversation.com/radical-overhaul-needed-to-halt-earths-sixth-great-extinction-event-68221
[25] Maxwell, et al, "Biodiversity"
[26] Laurance and Ehrlich, "Radical overhaul needed…"
[27] *Living Planet Report 2016*
[27] B Machovina, K Feeley and W Ripple, "Biodiversity conservation: The key is reducing meat consumption" *Science of the Total Environment* 2015 Dec 1;536:419-31
[28] Machovina, et al, "Biodiversity conservation'"
[29] See NT Wright *Surprised by Hope. Rethinking Heaven, the Resurrection, and the Mission of the Church* (HarperOne, 2008) and Middleton, *A New Heaven and a New Earth: Reclaiming Biblical Eschatology* (Baker Academic, 2014)
[30] Richard Bauckham, 2 Peter, Jude (Word Biblical Commentary 50, Word, 1983) 314-320
[31] IPCC, *Climate Change 2014. Synthesis Report Summary for Policy Makers* (IPCC 2014) p17
[32] Journalist's Resource, "How to mitigate climate change: Key facts from the U.N.'s 2014 report" Harvard Shorenstein Center Project (April 2014)
[33] World Health Organisation, Climate Change and Health Fact Sheet 2016. Accessed at http://www.who.int/mediacentre/factsheets/fs266/en/
[34] International Institute for Sustainable Development, "Climate Risk Management For Malaria Control In Kenya: The Case Of The Western Highlands" (2013)
[35] Environmental Justice Foundation, "Mangroves. Nature's Defence Against Tsunamis. A Report on the Impact of Mangrove Loss and Shrimp Farming on Coastal Defences" (2006)
[36] *Living Planet Report 2016*
[37] Walter Brueggeman, *Sabbath as Resistance. Saying No To The Culture Of Now* (Westminster John Knox Press 2014) p27

www.ingramcontent.com/pod-product-compliance
Lightning Source LLC
Chambersburg PA
CBHW070543300426
44113CB00011B/1778